The Primate Order

Family Trees

The Primate Order

R E B E C C A   S T E F O F F

 **Marshall Cavendish**
Benchmark
New York

With thanks to Toni E. Ziegler, Ph.D., Senior Scientist, National Primate Research Center and Department of Psychology, University of Wisconsin - Madison, for her expert review of this manuscript.

Marshall Cavendish Benchmark
99 White Plains Road
Tarrytown, New York 10591-9001
www.marshallcavendish.us

Library of Congress Cataloging-in-Publication Data

Stefoff, Rebecca, date.
The primate order / by Rebecca Stefoff.
p. cm. — (Family trees)
Includes bibliographical references and index.
ISBN 0-7614-1816-4
1. Primates—Juvenile literature. I. Title. II. Series.

QL737.P9S745 2005
599.8—dc22
2004021404

Front cover: Japanese macaques; Title page: Orangutans; Back cover: A mandrill

Photo research by Linda Sykes Picture Research
Mitsuaki Iwago/Minden Pictures: front cover, 28, 65; D. Robert & Lorri Franz/Corbis: 3; Frans Lanting/Minden Pictures: 6, 12 (left); 12 (right), 18, 22, 24, 32, 35, 48, 66; The Natural History Museum, London UK: 10; Keith Eskanos/Picturequest: 14 top right; Picturequest: 14 middle left; Burke/Triolo/Picturequest: 14 middle left; Jeff Schultz/Alaskan Express/Picturequest: 12 middle right; Martin Ruegner/Imagestate-Pictor/Picturequest: 15 bottom middle; Royalty-Free/Corbis: 14 top left; 14 middle center, 14 bottom left, 15 top right, 15 middle row (all), 15 bottom left; David Dennis/Animals Animals/Earth Scenes: 15 top left Sea World, Inc./ Corbis: 14 bottom right Swift/Vanuga Images/Corbis: 14 bottom row (middle); Photodisc/Getty Images: 14 bottom right, 15 bottom row, second from right, 15 bottom right; Toni Angermayer/Photo Researchers: 16; Claus Meyer/Minden Pictures: 17; John Reader/Photo Researchers: 21 (left); Patrick Robert/MPFT/ Corbis: 21 (right); Gerry Ellis/Minden Pictures: 25; Michael Dick/ Animals, Animals/Earth Scenes: 26; Karen Su/Corbis: 29, 54; Art Wolfe/Photo Researchers: 30, 61; Nigel Dennis/ Photo Researchers: 31; OSF/David Haring/Animals, Animals/Earth Scenes: 33 (bottom); Stephen Dalton/Photo Researchers: 33 (top); Gerard Lacz/Animals, Animals/Earth Scenes: 37; Claus Meyer/Minden Pictures: 38, 39, 56; Robert Pickett/Corbis: 40; Martin Harvey/Corbis: 41; Brandon D. Cole/Corbis: 42; David Northcott/Corbis: 43; Patrick Ward/Corbis: 44; Martin Harvey/Corbis: 45; D. Robert & Lorri Franz/Corbis: 46; Konrad Wothe/Minden Pictures: 50, 5, 601; Yann Arthus-Bertrand/Corbis: 55; L. & D. Klein/Photo Researchers: 58; T. Davis/Photo Researchers: 59; Gregory Dimijian, M. D./Photo Researchers: 63; S. Nagendra/Photo Researchers: 68; Theo Allofs/Corbis: 69; Nevada Wier/Corbis: 70; Language Research Center, Atlanta GA/Minden Pictures: 71; Christine & Juergen Sohns/Animals Animals/Earth Scenes: 72; Toni Angermayer/Photo Researchers: 73; Paulo Fridman/Corbis: 74; Bettmann/Corbis: 77; Mike Whittle/Ecoscene: 78; Peter Arnold, Inc.: 79; Gallo Images/Corbis: 80; Staffan Widstrand/Corbis: 85; Stocktrek/Corbis: back cover.

Series design by Patrice Sheridan

Printed in Malaysia
1 3 5 6 4 2

CONTENTS

A mouse lemur clings to a twig in Madagascar. One of the smallest and rarest primates, it is threatened with extinction because the forests where it lives are being cut down at a rapid rate.

Classifying Life

When night falls on the rainforests of northeastern Madagascar, a large island off the east coast of Africa, a small, shy creature called the mouse lemur cautiously creeps out of its hole high in a tree. Just a few inches long, the lemur weighs about the same as a mouse. It looks something like a mouse, with round ears, a pointed snout, and a long, narrow tail. Yet the lemur is more closely related to the huge mountain gorilla than to any mouse. Lemurs are primates, members of a large group of animals that includes the gorilla and other apes, all monkeys, the lemurs and their close kin—and human beings.

THE INVENTION OF TAXONOMY

To understand the connections among the primates, it helps to know something about how scientists classify living things. One of science's basic tasks is to provide tools for making sense of the natural world. Since ancient times, scientists who study life forms have worked on a powerful tool called classification. This is a way of organizing things in a pattern according to their differences and similarities. The classification of living things is called taxonomy. Through taxonomy, plants or animals that share certain features are grouped together and set apart from those with different features. Each group is then divided into smaller subgroups, and these in turn are split into still smaller groups. For example, plants form one group and animals form another group. Within the animal group are many smaller categories—birds, fish, mammals, and so on. And each of these categories could be subdivided in many ways.

Taxonomic classification seems simple, but the world of living things is complex and full of surprises. Taxonomy is not a fixed pattern but one that keeps changing to reflect new knowledge or ideas. Over time, however, scientists have agreed on a set of rules for adjusting that pattern even when they disagree on its details.

One of the first taxonomists was the ancient Greek philosopher Aristotle (384-322 B.C.E.), who turned his attention to many branches of science. From his writings on biology we know that he arranged living things on a sort of ladder, or scale, from those he considered lowest, or least developed, to those he thought of as highest, or most developed. A key element of Aristotle's system was dividing animals into those with backbones and those without backbones—a classification still used in modern taxonomy.

For centuries after Aristotle, taxonomy made little progress. People who studied nature tended to group organisms together by obvious features, such as separating trees from flowers or birds from fish. However, they did not try to develop a system for classifying all of life. Then, between 1682 and 1704, an English naturalist named John Ray published a plan of the living world designed to have a place for every species, or type, of plant and animal. Ray's system had several levels of larger and smaller categories. It was the foundation of modern taxonomy.

Swedish naturalist Carolus Linnaeus (1707-1778) built on that foundation to create the taxonomic system used today. Although Linnaeus's chief interest was plants, his system of classification included all living things. The highest level of classification was the kingdom, such as the plant or animal kingdom. Each kingdom was divided into classes. Each class was

The Many Levels of Classification

As biologists have learned more about living things, they have added levels of taxonomic classification to show newly understood similarities and differences. Here are the main taxonomic levels used today (each category includes the categories below it):

Kingdom
Phylum (for animals) or Division (for plants and fungi)
    Subphylum
Class
Order
    Suborder
    Infraorder
    Superfamily
Family
Genus
Species

This is an example of how a modern human would be classified:

Kingdom:	Animalia (animals)
Phylum:	Chordata (with spinal chords)
Subphylum:	Vertebrata (with segmented backbones)
Superclass:	Tetrapoda (with four limbs)
Class:	Mammalia (suckle young from mammary glands)
Subclass:	Theria (give birth to live young)
Infraclass:	Eutheria (young are contained in placenta)
Order:	Primata (most highly developed)
Superfamily:	Hominoidea (human-like)
Family:	Homindae (two-legged)
Genus:	*Homo* (human)
Species:	*sapiens* (modern human)

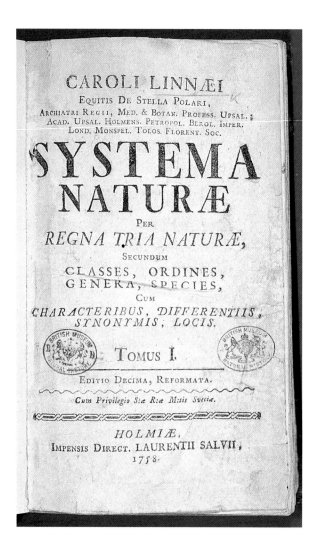

CAROLI LINNÆI

EQUITIS DE STELLA POLARI,

ARCHIATRI REGII, MED. & BOTAN. PROFESS. UPSAL.;
ACAD. UPSAL. HOLMENS. PETROPOL. BEROL. IMPER.
LOND. MONSPEL. TOLOS. FLORENT. SOC.

SYSTEMA
NATURÆ

PER

REGNA TRIA NATURÆ,

SECUNDUM

CLASSES, ORDINES,
GENERA, SPECIES,

CUM

CHARACTERIBUS, DIFFERENTIIS,
SYNONYMIS, LOCIS.

TOMUS I.

EDITIO DECIMA, REFORMATA.

Cum Privilegio S:æ R:æ M:tis Sveciæ.

HOLMIÆ,
IMPENSIS DIRECT. LAURENTII SALVII,
1758.

The *System of Nature*, as it is called in English, was one of the most important books in the history of science. Its plan for classifying all living things is still used today, although it has changed much since the eighteenth century.

divided into orders. Each order was divided into genera. Each genus (the singular form of genera) held one or more species.

Linnaeus also built on another idea from Ray: a method for naming species. Before Linnaeus published his important work *System of Nature* in 1735, there was no recognized scientific system for referring to plants and animals. Some organisms' common names were downright misleading—a jellyfish, for example, is not a fish. Many organisms were known by more than one name. Naturalists often called the same thing by different names, or used the same name for different things, which was confusing. Linnaeus established the practice of calling each plant or animal by its scientific name, which consists of the genus name and the species name, both in Latin, the scientific language of Linnaeus's day. For example, one of the two known species of mouse lemur has the scientific name *Microcebus murinus* (or *M. murinus* after the first time the full name is used). It belongs to the genus *Microcebus* and the species *murinus*.

Linnaeus did not classify the mouse lemur—scientists did not even know about that little animal until long after his death. But when they found the lemur, they could use Linnaeus's system to identify its place in the scheme of nature and give it a scientific name. Linnaeus's system could grow to include not only new species but new categories at all levels. It appeared at a time when European naturalists were exploring the rest of the world as never before, finding thousands of new plants and animals. This flood of discoveries was overwhelming at times, but Linnaean taxonomy helped scientists identify and organize their finds for systematic study.

MODERN TAXONOMY

Biologists still use the system of scientific naming that Linnaeus developed. Anyone who discovers a new species can choose its official species name, which must still be in Latin. Other aspects of taxonomy, though, have changed since Linnaeus's time.

The taxonomic structure grew more complex as scientists added new levels. The classification of an organism can now include a dozen or more taxonomic levels between kingdom and species. The information used to classify things has also changed. The earliest naturalists used obvious physical features, such as the differences between reptiles and mammals, to divide organisms into general groups. By the time of Ray and Linnaeus, naturalists were examining specimens in more detail. Aided by new tools such as the microscope, they explored the inner structures of plants and animals. For a long time after Linnaeus, classification was based mainly on details of anatomy, or physical structure, although scientists also looked at how an organism reproduced and how and where it lived.

Biologists can now peer more deeply into an organism's inner workings than Aristotle or Linnaeus ever dreamed possible. They can look

Ring-tailed lemurs from Madagascar (left) and a lowland gorilla from Central Africa (right) show the great variety of the primate order, a group that also includes humans.

inside its individual cells and study the arrangement of DNA that makes up its genetic blueprint. Genetic information is key to modern classification because DNA is more than an organism's blueprint—it also contains clues to how closely that organism is related to other species and how long ago those species separated during the process of evolution.

Taxonomic classifications change to reflect new information and new theories. In fact, there is no single, final taxonomy on which all scientists agree. Experts disagree on many points, such as whether or not organisms belong to the same species or to different species, or whether an organism represents a new species. Even at the highest level of classification scientists have various views. Some versions of taxonomy divide all life into four kingdoms, while others have as many as thirteen. Most taxonomies, however, divide life into five or six kingdoms: plants, animals, fungi, and kingdoms of tiny organisms such as bacteria, algae, and amoebas.

In recent years, a few biologists have suggested abandoning Linnaean taxonomy and scientific naming. They call for a new system based entirely on evolutionary relationships. True, the Linnaean system is a patchwork of old and new ideas. It does not clearly reflect the latest knowledge about evolutionary connections among creatures both living and extinct. So far, however, none of the proposed new systems has won wide acceptance from scientists. For all its shortcomings, the Linnaean system is still a handy and practical way for scientists—and teachers, nature writers, and students—to organize and share information about plants and animals. If scientists ever give up the Linnaean system, they will replace it with a different kind of taxonomy, because the urge to organize and classify things is the very root of science. Whatever method they use for drawing the branches and twigs, biologists will always be interested in the family tree of life.

Scientists classify living things in arrangements like this family tree of the anima

ANIMAL

PHYLA

CNIDARIANS

Coral

ARTHROPODS
(Animals with
external skeletons
and
jointed limbs)

MOLLUSKS

Octopus

**SUB
PHYLA**

CLASSES

CRUSTACEANS

Lobster

ARACHNIDS

Spider

INSECTS

Butterfly

MYRIAPODS

Centipede

ORDERS

CARNIVORES

Bear

SEA MAMMALS
(2 ORDERS)

Dolphin

PRIMATES

Monkey

kingdom to highlight the connections and the differences among the many forms of life.

KINGDOM

ANNELIDS

Earthworm

CHORDATES

(Animals
with a
dorsal
nerve chord)

ECHINODERMS

Starfish

VERTEBRATES

(Animals
with a
backbone)

FISH

Fish

BIRDS

Penguin

MAMMALS

AMPHIBIANS

Frog

REPTILES

Snake

HERBIVORES
(5 ORDERS)

Horse

RODENTS

Squirrel

INSECTIVORES

Hedgehog

MARSUPIALS

Kangaroo

SMALL MAMMALS
(SEVERAL ORDERS)

Rabbit

A young cotton-topped tamarin, clinging to its mother's back, peers at the world from beneath her mane of hair. Tamarins belong to a group of monkeys found in the Americas.

The Primates

In taxonomy, the primates are an order. Linnaeus gave them the Latin name Primata, meaning "chief" or "uppermost," because he thought they were the most highly developed or advanced of all animals.

The taxonomic classification of primates begins with the kingdom Animalia, which includes all animals. The next level of classification is the phylum Chordata, animals that have spinal cords. The subphylum is Vertebrata, animals with backbones made of bones called vertebrae. The next level down is the superclass Tetrapoda, vertebrates with four limbs. Below that is the class Mammalia, tetrapods that are warm-blooded and suckle their young from the mother's body. The next level is the subclass Theria, mammals that give birth to live young. The infraclass Eutheria includes animals whose young are enclosed in a membrane called a placenta before birth. Placental mammals are divided into a number of orders. One of those orders is the primates.

PRIMATE ORIGINS

The image of a family tree fits the primates especially well because most primate species, past and present, have lived in tropical forests. Many have been arboreal, which means they spend most of their time in trees. Primates'

forest-dwelling ways have made life tough for scientists who want to trace primates' origins through the fossilized remains of their ancestors. Tropical forests
are not ideal environments for turning animal skeletons into fossils. They do
not usually have sand, mud, or volcanic ash that can cover the remains before
other animals take them apart and devour them. As a result, scientists have
found fewer fossils of primates than of many other groups. About two-thirds
of the primate fossils they *do* have are single teeth or small pieces of bone.

Paleontologists who study the fossil record think that primates have
been around for about 60 million years. Primates evolved from ancient
insect-eating mammals that resembled treeshrews, small creatures alive
today. The oldest primate fossil comes from Purgatory Hill in Montana. It
is the tooth of an extinct animal scientists call *Purgatorius,* which was about
the size of a mouse.

In recent years, though, some scientists have challenged the paleonto-
logical view. Using mathematics instead of fossils, a team of researchers at
the Field Museum in Chicago developed a formula based on the number of
living primate species, the number of known extinct primate species, and
the estimated survival time of the average species (2.5 million years).

A treeshrew in Borneo, Southeast Asia. Early primates probably looked much like treeshrews.

PRIMATE EVOLUTION

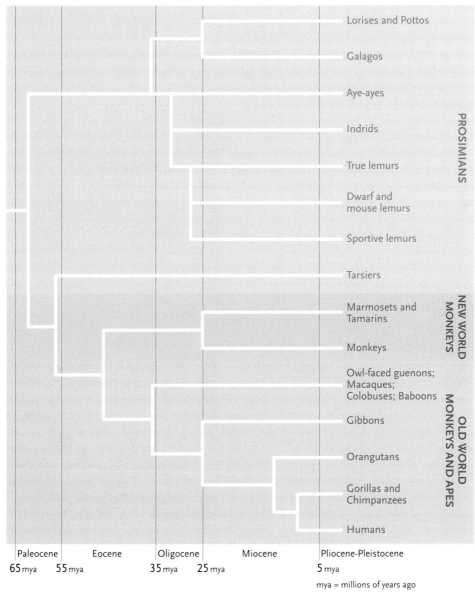

Most experts now think that the ancestors of modern primates appeared between 65 and 55 million years ago, although new discoveries could change that view. Our understanding of primate evolution grows constantly through scientific work in fossil fields and in laboratories.

Finding a Place on the Family Tree

One of the most exciting and controversial areas of science is the study of the origins and evolution of *Homo sapiens,* the modern human. Scientists know that human beings are primates and are most closely related to the apes. But they do not yet know the details of how and when humans evolved.

English naturalist Charles Darwin was the first to describe evolution at length and to explain how it could have taken place. His books, *On the Origin of Species* (1859) and *The Descent of Man* (1871), caused a sensation. They were particularly disturbing to people who did not want to recognize that humans are part of the natural world and the animal kingdom. Some ridiculed Darwin for saying that people were descended from monkeys or apes. What Darwin really said is that humans and anthropoids were both descended from some unknown, shared ancestor in the distant past. Science has proved him correct. A series of spectacular fossil finds—such as the remains of European Neandertals, who lived at the same time as early modern humans, and the fossil skeleton known as "Lucy," who lived in East Africa some 3.5 million years ago—have introduced us to our recent cousins and our remote ancestors.

Lucy, the Neandertals, and modern humans, along with many other extinct species, are hominids, "humanlike" primates. Humans and their ancestors share several key features. They walk upright on two feet at all times, and their brains tend to be larger in relation to their bodies than those of other primates. The hominids split off from the line of African apes, but when? Estimates range from six million to fifteen million years ago. Many kinds of early hominids evolved after that split. Scientists do not know for sure which group gave rise to the genus *Homo,* which contains both the extinct Neandertals and modern humans.

Each new fossil find in the field of human origins sparks debate. In July 2002, for example, paleontologists working in the North African country of Chad announced the discovery of a skull that is six to seven million years old. They believe it to be hominid, the oldest human ancestor yet found. Some scientists, though, think that the fossil is really the skull of an ancient ape. The fossil skull, nicknamed Toumai, will be the focus of study for years to come. It and other relics of ancient primates and hominids—along with fossils yet to be discovered—will one day help us fill in the blanks in our own family tree.

In 1974, scientists working in Ethiopia found the fossil remains of one of the earliest known human ancestors—a female hominid from about 3.5 million years ago. They nicknamed her Lucy, but her scientific name is *Australopithecus afarensis*. She is one of the most complete hominid fossils ever found. Scientists recovered 40 percent of her skeleton, giving them enough information to say that she was female, about twenty years old when she died, and no more than 4 feet (120 centimeters) tall.

The Toumai skull contains clues about the early history of humans and their primate relatives. Scientists are still investigating whether it is the oldest human ancestor yet discovered or an ancient, extinct ape.

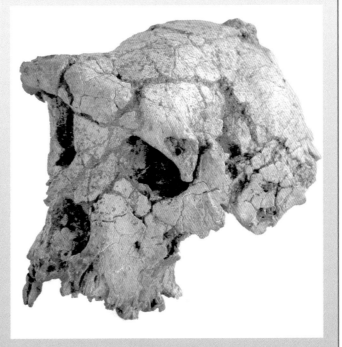

In 2002 they announced that, according to their calculations, the ancestor of all primates probably emerged between 85 and 80 million years ago. Many paleontologists disagreed, arguing that no fossils support the new date. Researchers continue to investigate the question of when primates first appeared.

By about 55 million years ago, evolution had produced two groups of early primates, the Adapidae and the Omomyidae. These two groups were different from earlier tree-dwelling mammals, with characteristics closer to those of modern primates. Their brains were larger, their eyes bigger, and their snouts shorter and less rodentlike than those of *Purgatorius* and its immediate descendants. These changes show that the adapids and omomyids made more use of sight and less use of scent than their ancestors. Their feet had changed, too. Flat nails had replaced claws on some toes. The adapids and omomyids had also developed opposable toes. The first toe on each foot was set apart from the other toes and could curl in the opposite direction, like the thumb on a human hand. With opposable toes, these arboreal primates could grasp branches securely.

Paleontologists and taxonomists have not yet settled the question of how the adapids and omomyids developed into the many groups of later primates. Most think that the adapids gave rise to lemurs and their close kin, while the omomyids gave rise to monkeys, apes, and small Asian primates called tarsiers. During the 1990s, however, some researchers suggested that monkeys and apes descended from an unknown third group of early primates. Scientists are now studying

The hands of two primates: a human being and a sifaka, a type of lemur.

recent fossil finds from China and Egypt in the hope of learning more about where, when, and how monkeys and apes first evolved.

Between 35 and 5 million years ago, many kinds of primates appeared around the world. Most of them became extinct. The ancestors of all modern primates had come into existence between 8 and 5 million years ago. Some species that descended from them disappeared, leaving only fossil traces, but others survived and evolved into today's primates.

PRIMATES TODAY

Approximately 280 species of primates live in the world today, mostly in tropical or subtropical zones. Another thirty or forty species became extinct during the past few thousand years.

Traditionally, zoologists divided the order of primates into two suborders, the prosimians and the anthropoids. The prosimian suborder included all primates other than monkeys and apes. Its main groups were lorises, galagos, tarsiers, and several categories of lemurs. Prosimians were sometimes called the primitive or lower primates because they resemble the ancient, ancestral primates in structure. The anthropoid suborder, or higher primates, included monkeys, apes, and humans. (Some scientists kept the traditional prosimian and anthropoid suborders but classified tarsiers in a third suborder of their own.)

The terms prosimian and anthropoid, or lower and higher primate, can be useful for talking or writing about primates. Many experts, however, no longer use these terms as scientific categories. Instead, they divide primates into two suborders called the Strepsirhini and the Haplorhini. The Strepsirhini suborder contains all of the prosimians except tarsiers. The Haplorhini suborder contains tarsiers, monkeys, apes, and humans. These suborders are defined by the anatomy of the nose and upper lip. All strepsirhines have moist nostrils surrounded by hairless skin. A division beneath their noses splits their upper lips into two halves. Haplorhines

The aye-aye belongs to the subgroup primates called strepsirhines. All of the primates in this group have moist noses and split, or divided, upper lips.

have dry noses, hairs on their noses or in their nostrils, and smooth, undivided upper lips.

The number of families in each suborder differs from one taxonomist to another. Most divide the strepsirhines into six or seven families. Where haplorhines are concerned, everyone agrees on one family of tarsiers, and most experts group monkeys into four families. Putting apes and humans into families, however, is a matter of dispute.

Traditionally, gibbons and siamangs, sometimes called the lesser apes, went into a family called the Hylobatids. The great apes—chimpanzees, bonobos, gorillas, and orangutans—went into the Pongid family. Humans had their own family, the Hominids. Some scientists still accept this classification. Recent genetic research, however, has shown that humans are more closely related to some species of apes than the ape species are to each other. Humans and chimpanzees, for example, share between 95 and 99 percent of their genetic makeup—more than chimps and gibbons share. Because of these findings, some zoologists have reclassified apes and humans. One new system eliminates the Pongid family, placing the great apes with humans in the Hominids. Another classification also combines great apes and humans into one family but calls them all Pongids, eliminating the Hominid family. Time will tell which system gains wider use.

All primates share certain general features. Their eyes are placed at the front of their heads, facing forward. Primates cannot see as far around

The chimpanzee is a member of the haplorhine suborder of primates. Haplorhines have dry noses and smooth, undivided upper lips. Humans belong to this primate suborder.

them as animals with eyes on the sides of their heads, such as horses. However, their two eyes' fields of vision overlap. This gives primates good depth perception, the ability to judge distance—a useful trait in animals that jump or climb from tree to tree. Primates also have hair on all or part of their faces and bodies (humans are the least hairy primates). They have five digits on each hand or foot. Their flexible fingers and toes, with opposable digits, make it easy for them to grasp branches when climbing or perching. Anthropoids have especially sensitive and mobile digits, and can easily handle and manipulate all kinds of things. Some monkeys also have tails that are flexible, delicate organs of touch. Such a limb, called a prehensile tail, can grasp a branch as well as a hand does. Primate females devote a fairly large percentage of their time to rearing their young. In many species, the young mature slowly and need a lot of care and

Tarsiers' body shapes and habits are much like those of galagos and lemurs, which are strepsirhines. But tarsiers' noses and upper lips are like those of monkeys and apes, the haplorhines. Most scientists place tarsiers in the haplorhine suborder, but they also consider them to be prosimians, a category that includes all primates other than monkeys, apes, and humans.

education from their mothers in order to survive. Finally, primates are among the most intelligent and social animals. Most species live in groups, and some form highly organized communities with complex social interactions. And a few primates do things once thought possible only for humans—they make tools, use languages, and even wage war on their own species.

One important feature of primates is their brains, which have more ability to store information than those of most other animals. Primate brains also have complex, interconnected structures for memory and various kinds of thinking. These flexible brains make primates good learners, which helps them adapt to life in a wide variety of circumstances.

Although primates share some common characteristics, they also differ dramatically, as in the case of the mouse lemur and the mountain gorilla. Prosimians, monkeys, and apes all have distinctive features and a wide array of species. Primates, in fact, are a very diverse and colorful order. The fact that they are our closest relatives is only one of the things that makes them so fascinating.

A pygmy marmoset in Peru, South America. Pygmy marmosets are the world's smallest monkeys, weighing less than a quarter of a pound (3.5 ounces or 100 grams).

Primate Families and Physical Features

People live almost everywhere on earth, but nonhuman primates are found only in Africa, Asia, and Central and South America. In each continent they inhabit a broad band of land with the Equator at its center. The northern limit of the primate range runs through Japan, East Asia, North Africa, and southern Mexico. The southern limit runs through Indonesia, South Africa, and northern Argentina, southern Brazil, and Paraguay in South America. Other than captive and zoo animals, the only primates that live outside these limits are small colonies introduced by humans in a few places. Within the overall range of the primates, strepsirhines, tarsiers, monkeys, and apes have their own geographic territories and physical characteristics.

STREPSIRHINES

Strepsirhines, or lemurs and their kin, are found only in Africa and Asia. In addition to their moist nostrils and hairless noses, they share other features. Nearly all strepsirhines have a dental comb, a set of lower front teeth adapted for grooming their fur. In many strepsirhines, the second digit of each hind foot has evolved into a long claw called the toilet claw, also used in grooming. Most strepsirhines are arboreal, spending all or most of their time in trees, although a few species also forage on the ground. Many strepsirhines have long hind legs to propel them as they leap among trees and branches. Almost all of them have tails, which the leaping and jumping species use to balance themselves as they run along branches or leap through the air. One widely used classification divides strepsirhines into seven families: five of lemurs, one of galagos, and one of lorises.

The lemurs are the largest and most diverse group of strepsirhines. All lemurs live on the large Indian Ocean island of Madagascar, near Africa. The five lemur families are dwarf and mouse lemurs, true lemurs, sportive or weasel lemurs, indrids, and aye-ayes. Dwarf and mouse lemurs are among the smallest primates, with bodies ranging in length from 4.9 to 10.7 inches (125 to 272 millimeters). Their tails are one to one-and-a-half times as long as their bodies. All dwarf and mouse lemurs are arboreal and nocturnal.

True lemurs are diurnal, which means that they are active by day. They move through trees either by running along branches or by leaping, and some species also move about on the ground. Most true lemurs are about the size of a house cat. They range in length from 11 to 17.8 inches

Ruffed lemur, Madagascar.

(280-452 millimeters), with tails as long as their bodies, or longer. Lemurs have thick coats of dense, plushy fur, with very thick fur on their tails. Some species also have tufts of fur on the tips of their ears or ruffs around their necks. Their coats can be white, gray, brown, reddish-brown, or black in color. Many have vivid markings, such as the white face mask and black-and-white-striped tail of the ring-tailed lemur, or the black-and-white patchwork of the ruffed lemur. Females of some species are smaller than males or have different coloring.

The sportive or weasel lemurs are closely related to a very large extinct lemur called *Megaladapis,* which weighed between 88 and 176 pounds (40 and 80 kilograms)! This bulky, short-legged lemur, which probably looked and acted something like an oversized koala, became extinct a few thousand years ago. Its surviving relatives are much smaller, weighing just one or two pounds (17.5 to 31.5 ounces, 500 to 900 grams). They have brown or gray backs, white bellies, and long hind legs that make them powerful jumpers.

The indrid family consists of five lemur species: the indri, the avahi, and three types of sifakas. The indri is the largest strepsirhine, with a body length of 24 to 35 inches (610 to 900 millimeters) and a weight of 13 to 22 pounds (6 to 10 kilograms). Its tail, however, is short—little more than a stump. The avahi is much smaller. The fur on its body and long tail is short and so dense that the animal is sometimes

Verreaux's sifaka, Madagascar.

31

called the woolly lemur. The sifakas are midway between the indri and the avahi in size. Their bodies are 17.5 to 21.5 inches (450 to 550 millimeters) long, with tails of equal length, and they weigh 6.6 to 15.4 pounds (3 to 7 kilograms). Slender, long-legged, and graceful, sifakas have white, tan, brown, gray, or black masklike patterns on their faces and heads.

The fifth lemur family contains only one species, *Daubentonia madagascariensis*, called the aye-aye. One of the rarest primates, the aye-aye is about 15.5 inches in body length, with a tail longer than its body. It weighs around 5.5 pounds (2.5 kilograms). Aye-ayes do not leap and cling like other lemurs. Instead, they creep through the trees on all four legs. Aye-ayes are the only strepsirhines without a dental comb, but they do have two unique features. One is a pair of square, chisel-like upper front teeth, much like those of rodents. Aye-ayes use these teeth to gnaw through the bark and wood of trees, looking for insect larvae. The third digit on each front foot has evolved into a long claw for pulling the larvae out of the holes.

The aye-aye is one of the rarest primates. It is a kind of lemur, but it has a feature that no other lemurs possess. The third toe on each of the aye-aye's front feet has evolved into a tool for digging larvae, or grubs, out of the bark of trees.

Flash photography captures a *Galago senegalensis,* or lesser bushbaby, leaping from branch to branch. Galagos are champion primate leapers. Their long hind legs act like springs, propelling them forward with great energy.

The remaining two families of strepsirhines are galagos and lorises. The dozen or so species of galagos, also called bushbabies, live in Africa. They range in size from the dwarf bushbaby, weighing 2 ounces (60 grams), to the thick-tailed bushbaby, which can weigh as much as 2.6 pounds (1.2 kilograms). Galagos are slender, nimble, fast-moving tree-dwellers with long tails. Their hind legs are significantly longer than their front legs and act as springs for great leaps from branch to branch. Bushbabies have been known to jump as far as 39 feet (12 meters).

Slender loris. Members of the loris family have opposable thumbs and big toes that give them a secure grasp on tree branches. Lorises are nocturnal and their large eyes gather enough light for night vision.

Their "fingertips" and "toetips" are flat, disklike pads that help them grip and stick to branches. Galagos have toilet claws, but they do not have opposable thumbs and big toes as lemurs do. Their large ears can move in all directions to pick up sounds.

The loris family contains two types of small, arboreal primates with a weight range slightly greater than that of galagos. Pottos, including a species sometimes called an angwantibo, live in Central and West Africa, while lorises are Asian. The slender loris is native to India and Sri Lanka. The slow loris is found in India, Southeast Asia, and the Philippines. The limbs of pottos and lorises are shorter than those of galagos. Instead of running and leaping, members of the loris family climb through trees with a methodical, hand-over-hand motion. Opposable thumbs and big toes give these nocturnal animals a strong grip, allowing them to sleep all day while clinging to a branch if they cannot find a convenient hole in a tree. Lorises and pottos have very short tails or none at all.

TARSIERS

Tarsiers are small nocturnal primates found on the Southeast Asian islands of Indonesia and the Philippines. Excellent jumpers, with long hindlimbs and short forelimbs, tarsiers range in length from 3.3 to 6.2 inches (85 to 160 millimeters). Their tails are longer than their bodies and hairless except for tufts near the end. Their ears are also almost hairless, and quite flexible— tarsiers move their ears constantly, even folding and crinkling them. Their eyes, however, are fixed in their sockets and cannot roll from side to side like those of all other primates. Tarsiers make up for this by being able to turn their heads very far around in each direction to see what is on either side and behind them.

Tarsiers have been called prosimians, along with the lemurs, galagos, and lorises. Like galagos, tarsiers have pads on their fingers and toes. Their movements and nocturnal way of life are much like those of galagos and some

Note the pads on the fingers and toes of this Western tarsier from Borneo.

lemurs. Scientists now believe, however, that early in primate evolution the ancestors of tarsiers split off from the line leading to lemurs, galagos, and lorises. Tarsiers also share some key features, such as hairy skin around the nostrils and an undivided upper lip, with monkeys and apes. For this reason many experts now classify tarsiers as haplorhines, along with monkeys and apes.

MONKEYS

More than half of all primates species are monkeys. All monkeys belong to the suborder Haplorhini, but they are divided into two smaller categories called infraorders. The platyrrhines, or broad-nosed monkeys, have widely separated nostrils that open to the sides. They are sometimes called the New World monkeys because they are found only in the Americas. The catarrhines, or narrow-nosed monkeys, are known as Old World monkeys because they are native to Africa and Asia. Their nostrils are close together and open downward, like those of apes (which are also catarrhines). Another feature unique to catarrhine monkeys is that some species have ischial callosities—pads of tough, hairless skin, which may be brightly colored, on their rumps or around their sexual organs. Scientists think ischial

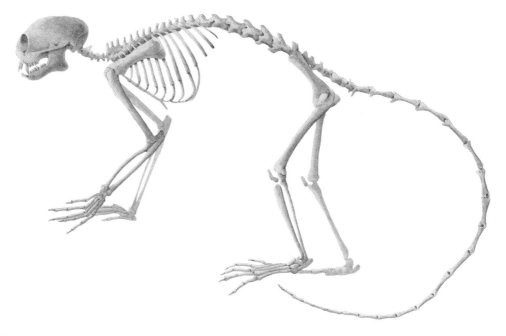

The marmoset's tail—as long as its body—helps it balance and move through trees. All of the bones are small and slender, like the marmoset itself. Small size and light weight are advantages for these tree-dwellers.

callosities evolved for comfortable sitting on the ground and also to attract sexual partners.

There are three families of New World monkeys: callitrichids, atelids, and cebids. The callitrichid family consists of several dozen species known as marmosets and tamarins. These primates live in tropical forests. Most tamarins are found from Costa Rica as far south as the Amazon River, while most marmosets live south of the Amazon. Tamarins and marmosets are small, with bodies 5 to 14.4 inches (130 to 370 millimeters) long and tails one-and-a-half times as long. The world's smallest monkey, the pygmy marmoset, weighs 3.5 ounces (100 grams), but other callitrichid species can weigh up to nine times as much. Marmosets and tamarins are diurnal runners and leapers. They have long hands and feet, like squirrels, but lack opposable thumbs and toes. Their digits end in claws rather than flattened nails, except for the large toe on each foot, which has a flattened nail. The hair of marmosets and tamarins is soft and silky, and some species have prominent patches of long fur on or near their faces, forming manes, mustaches, ear tufts, or neck ruffs.

The cebid family contains the smaller-bodied New World monkeys, including capuchin and squirrel monkeys. The smallest species, the night or owl monkey, has a body length of 9.4 inches

Emperor tamarin. Many species of tamarins and marmosets have silky, distinctive plumes or tufts of fur.

(240 millimeters). The atelid family contains larger-bodied monkeys, such as howler, spider, and woolly monkeys. The largest atelids are various species of woolly and spider monkeys, which can be 35.7 inches (915 millimeters) long. Cebids and atelids are almost entirely arboreal, and nearly all are active only by day. The only nocturnal species is the well-named night or owl monkey.

All cebids and atelids have long limbs and curved, flattened nails rather than claws. They have opposable big toes, but their thumbs are not opposable and are extremely small or even nonexistent in some species. The tails of almost all species are long and furry. Spider, howler, and woolly monkeys have prehensile tails, which have bare patches of sensitive skin on their undersides. The muriqui, another atelid, also has a prehensile tail. The monkeys use these tails as extra hands for touching and grasping. Scientists have discovered that the exposed skin on prehensile tails has markings that are as individual as fingerprints.

The muriqui, also called the woolly spider monkey, is one of many species of New World monkeys that have sensitive, flexible tails called prehensile tails. Monkeys use prehensile tails as extra hands for grasping objects or hanging from branches.

Some cebids and atelids have distinctive coloring. The white-faced capuchin is dark brown or black, with the obvious exception of its face. The black-handed spider monkey can be any shade from gold through red to brown, with black markings on its hands, head, and tail. The coloring of black howler monkeys depends upon their gender, a condition that scientists call sexual dichromatism. All young black howler monkeys have hair of a creamy gray color, but the males turn black when they reach adulthood. The white-faced saki, a medium-sized monkey found in the Amazon River basin, also exhibits sexual dichromatism. Females are dark brown or black, with reddish hair on their lower bellies. Adult males are black except for their faces, which are covered with short, stiff, off-white hair. The three species of uakaris, closely related to the saki species, are yellow or red, and two of them have hairless, bright red heads and faces.

Golden-faced saki from Brazil's Amazon region display what scientists call sexual dichromatism, which means that males and females are physically different. In the case of the saki, the difference is in the color and fullness of the hair. The male is on the left, the female on the right.

Goeldi's monkey.

One New World primate, Goeldi's monkey, is a challenge to taxonomists. Although its teeth are like those of the cebids, its body and digits resemble those of a marmoset. Most zoologists place Goeldi's monkey with the marmosets in the callitrichid family, but a few classify it in a family of its own.

The Old World monkeys, or cercopithecids, form the largest family in the primate order, with approximately ninety species. They are divided into two subfamilies, colobines and cercopithecines. Colobines have distinctive anatomical features related to their diet. They are entirely vegetarian. Most are largely folivorous, which means that they eat leaves. Leaves contain more tough fiber and less nutrition than other plant parts such as fruits and nuts. They require lengthy digestion, so colobines have evolved large stomachs divided into several chambers. On the other hand, cercopithecines eat almost anything but leaves, and they have smaller, one-chambered stomachs. They also have cheek pouches in which they can store food temporarily, and their eyes are closer together than those of colobines.

Colobines, or leaf-eating monkeys, fall into five groups. One group is the colobus monkeys, which lack thumbs. They live in the forests of Central, West, and East Africa. The largest, the black and white colobus, weighs between 15 and 32 pounds (7 and 15 kilograms); the olive colobus is the smallest, at 6.5 to 8.8 pounds (3 to 4 kilograms).

All other colobine monkeys live in Asia. Langurs are found throughout India and Southeast Asia. One species, the hanuman langur, is sacred to followers of the Hindu religion and is often seen around temples and in villages. Langurs have small thumbs. They are arboreal, but they also search for food on the ground, spending more time there than any other colobine. Proboscis monkeys, another type of Asian colobine, live on the Southeast Asian island of Borneo. Proboscis means "nose," and this monkey's most notable feature is its large, drooping nose, bigger in males than in females. Males, in fact, are bigger generally, weighing up to 52 pounds (24 kilograms), about twice as much as the typical female. Another colobine, the snub-nosed or golden monkey, lives high in the mountains of southern and western China. Its scientific name is *Rhinopithecus roxellana* and refers to Roxellana, the wife of a long-ago emperor. Legend says that she laughed a lot, and the snub-nosed monkey's expression can give it the appearance of smiling or laughing. The last of the leaf-eaters is the douc monkey, which lives in Southeast Asia. About the size of a langur, it is dark gray with a yellow face, a white beard, and white tail and hands.

A proboscis monkey. These leaf-eating Southeast Asian monkeys are named for their most noticeable feature—proboscis means "nose."

The black-and-white primate species often referred to as DeBrazza's monkey is a kind of guenon. It is found in many zoos around the world.

The cercopithecine monkeys fall into six groups. Five of these groups are found only in Africa. The largest group includes many kinds of monkeys from many parts of the continent, such as guenons, vervets, and red forest monkeys. Guenons are the most common monkeys in Africa. These small primates live in forests, open woodlands, and savannahs south of the Sahara Desert. Some species spend much time on the ground, but all are basically arboreal, balancing with their long tails as they leap from tree to tree. Talapoins, which swim well and take to the water when chased by predators, also belong to this group. They are the smallest Old World monkeys, weighing 2 to 3 pounds (1.3 to 1.8 kilograms).

Another group includes the patas monkeys, which live in open woodlands and savannahs south of the Sahara. Long-limbed and sleek, they run on all fours and are the fastest-moving primates in the world, reaching speeds of 35 miles (56 kilometers) an hour. Another group, the mangabeys, are medium-sized monkeys that live in high in the treetops. They inhabit the rainforests of Central and West Africa. Baboons and mandrills are large monkeys with long muzzles and long, sharp canine teeth—which is why people have called them "dog-faced" ever since Aristotle's time. They spend a lot of time on the ground, moving nimbly on four legs, but they climb

Hamadryas baboons are native to Egypt. Ancient Egyptians admired baboons, which they thought were sacred to the god Thoth. Hamadryas baboons appear in many artworks created by the ancient Eygptians. Wall paintings in ancient tombs suggest that some Egyptians kept baboons as pets, or at least encouraged them to live in their gardens.

swiftly into trees or up cliffs when danger threatens. The two species of mandrill, called the mandrill and the drill, live in West Africa. The five species of baboon are distributed across much of Africa, from southern Egypt and Mali in the north to South Africa. One species, the hamadryas baboon of Egypt and the western Sahara, is also found in Saudi Arabia. It was taken there by humans within the past 4,000 years. The fifth group of cercopithecine monkeys is the geladas, which live in high, dry country in Ethiopia and East Africa. They have manes and red eyes and are similar to baboons.

The sixth group of cercopithecine species is the macaques. These monkeys have the widest geographic range of any primate, other than humans. Macaques are found across Africa and Asia, from Morocco to Japan, and are at home both in trees and on the ground. Two species, the

A Barbary macaque in Gibraltar. This colony of monkeys is sometimes mistakenly called the Barbary apes. Tradition says that when the macaques leave Gibraltar, the British will also leave.

Barbary macaque and the Celebes black macaque, are the only Old World monkeys without tails. Barbary macaques are native to North Africa, but for several hundred years a transplanted colony of them has lived in Gibraltar, a British colony on the Spanish peninsula, where they are sometimes called "Barbary apes." Another species, the rhesus macaque, is used in medical testing throughout much of the world, although laboratory animals generally come from captive breeding colonies, not wild populations.

APES

Like Old World monkeys, apes are catarrhine or narrow-nosed primates within the suborder Haplorhini. Apes are tailless and larger than most monkeys. Like monkeys, they usually walk on all fours. Apes, however, can also stand and walk on two legs, and they sometimes do so.

The apes are divided into two families. The eleven species in the hylobatid family are the gibbons and siamangs, sometimes called the lesser apes. They live in the forests of eastern India, southeastern China, and Southeast Asia. Siamangs weigh 22 to 27 pounds (10 to 12 kilograms). Gibbons are smaller, about 11 to 16 pounds (5 to 7 kilograms). Some of the lesser apes have throat sacs, pouches of flesh that fill with air to give the animals a loud, resonating call. The hylobatids have long arms and long, slender, hands and feet. They are entirely arboreal and move through the trees by brachiating, which means swinging forward from their hands, first right and then left. Gibbons and siamangs have a special joint in their wrists that lets them rotate their bodies while they swing, so that they can reach in any direction for their next grip without losing hold of the branch from which they are hanging. Other leaping primates sometimes hang from their hands as they travel, but only the hylobatids use the swinging, rotating movement of true brachiation.

White-handed gibbon, Southeast Asia.

The remaining nonhuman primates are the four species of great apes. All have opposable thumbs and big toes with flattened nails. Only one species, the orangutan, lives in Asia. Once it inhabited much of Southeast Asia, but today it is limited to a few places on the islands of Sumatra and Borneo. Orangutans spend nearly all of their time in the trees. Although they sometimes hang from their hands and feet, they tend to move slowly and do not travel with the swift, turning, hand-over-hand swing of brachiation. On the ground orangs walk on all fours, with their feet flat but their hands clenched. Adult males weigh from 100 to 220 pounds (45 to 100 kilograms). Females are somewhat smaller. A typical male orang has a head and body length of 4.1 to 4.9 feet (1.25 to 1.5 meters). Its arms are long relative to its legs—when it stands, its arms reach to its ankles. Orangs have shaggy, somewhat sparse hair that ranges from brown to reddish.

An orangutan carries her young through a Sumatran rain forest. This ape's name is said to mean "hairy man of the forest" in a Southeast Asian language.

The remaining three species of great apes are found only in Africa. *Pan paniscus,* the pygmy chimpanzee or bonobo, is native to a region in the Democratic Republic of the Congo (the Central African nation formerly known as Zaire). *Pan troglodytes,* the true or common chimpanzee, lives in forests throughout Central Africa from Senegal in the west to Uganda in the east. When standing, chimpanzees are about 3.3 to 5.6 feet tall (1 to 1.7 meters). Males weigh between 75 and 154 pounds (34 and 70 kilograms). Females are about two-thirds as large. Bonobos are only slightly smaller. Both species place the knuckles of their hands, rather than their fists, on the ground when they walk. They sometimes hang or swing from their arms, but they do not brachiate.

The gorilla is the largest of the primates. The bony crest on the top of its skull serves as an attachment point for long, strong jaw muscles that let the gorilla chew tough plants.

The final great ape is known to science as *Gorilla gorilla*. There are three subspecies, each with a separate geographic range. The western lowland gorilla lives in West and Central Africa. The eastern lowland gorilla lives in East Africa. The mountain gorilla is found high on six volcanic peaks of the Virunga range in east-central Africa. The gorilla is the largest primate, with a strong, stocky body and thick limbs. Males typically stand 4.1 to 5.8 feet tall (1.25 to 1.75 meters) and weigh 340-370 pounds (155 to 165 kilograms)—and captive gorillas often weigh considerably more than that. Females are about half the size of males. Because gorillas have broad chests and long arms, the distance from one hand to the other when they stretch their arms out to the sides is greater than their height. Like chimpanzees, gorillas usually walk and run on feet and knuckles, but they can move around upright. They sometimes stand tall to see over vegetation or to make themselves look big to other animals. Their hair is generally dark,

Lowland gorillas, Africa.

Primate Facts

Primate	Average Weight* (pounds)	Gestation Period (days)	Reproductive Age** (years)	Average Lifespan (years)
Orangutan	88	275	11.75	32
Chimpanzee	66	224	14	41
Baboon	28.6	184	6.5	28.5
Langur	25.5	168	4	20
Rhesus Macaque	15.2	168	3.5	25
Woolly Monkey	12.7	180	4.5	12
Gibbon	12	210	8	33
Long-tailed Macaque	9	165	4.75	27
Ring-tailed lemur	6	132	3	27
Squirrel Monkey	1.3	133	3.5	21
Gallago (bushbaby)	0.44	120	1.5	9
Tamarin	1.1	134–184	2	15

*Average weight given is for females. In some species, males often weigh more.

**Reproductive age is the age at which a female typically begins mating and bearing young.

but mature males, called "silverbacks," develop bands or patches of gray or white across their backs. Despite their impressive size and strength, gorillas are generally peace-loving primates. They spend most of their time sitting quietly on the ground, eating.

An Angola colobus, one of Africa's leaf-eating monkeys. Colobus monkeys spend much of their time in trees, foraging for food.

Habitat and Diet

An organism's physical structure reveals the evolutionary history that shaped it. So does its way of life. The evolutionary history of primates unfolded largely above the ground. Primates adapted to life in the trees, and most of them still live there. The habitats they occupy and the foods they eat reflect their arboreal origins.

PRIMATES AT HOME

Except for adult gorillas, nearly all primates spend some or all of their time in trees. Many species almost never walk along the ground. Primates travel in three dimensions. Moving up or down is as natural to them as moving north, south, east, or west.

Whether in the Americas, Africa, or Asia, the majority of primate species live in tropical rainforests. A rainforest offers certain advantages to arboreal animals that are active all year. Some strepsirhines sleep in holes in trees, and a few haplorhines make nests of leaves or grasses, but most primates spend all their time in the open. The tropics have a stable climate, without the big shifts in temperature between winter and summer that other climates experience. The main seasonal shifts are between rainy and dry seasons. Primates are well able to endure rain, and the trees in which they spend much of their time offer some protection.

As a habitat, tropical rainforests can be remarkably varied, with many vegetation zones. These include cool, damp cloud forests on tropical mountains; swamp forests; gallery forests with little underbrush and high canopies of foliage; understory forests thick with brush and vines; and heath forests with sparse trees or shrubs on sandy soil. Several species may live in the same locality in this varied habitat. Sometimes different species use the same resources, which are abundant enough to support all. A 190-square-mile (500-square-kilometer) tract of rainforest in Peru, for example, has been found to contain at least twenty-two species of New World monkeys. At least thirteen of them forage for the same foods—mainly fruit and insects—in the lowland forest around a single lake.

In other cases, though, different primate species live together without competing directly for resources because they are adapted to living in different parts of the forest, to being active at different times, and to eating different foods. The M'Passa Plateau in Gabon, West Africa, for example, is home to five nocturnal species of prosimians and about a dozen diurnal anthropoids, including talapoins, drills, and chimpanzees. Some of the monkeys forage high in the treetops, others in lower branches. The talapoins stick close to water, while the drills and chimpanzees are often found at the edges of open patches of scrub or grassland. In South Africa, two species of bushbabies occupy the same forest, but one eats dragonflies and beetles while the other preys on ants, termites, and centipedes.

In tropical regions with multiple primate species, some monkeys forage in mixed-species groups. Squirrel and capuchin monkeys often associate with one another in Central and South America. In Africa, various species of guenons and mangabeys are often found together. Outside tropical forests, though, mixed-species associations are rare. Open woodlands and savannahs have fewer primate species and scarcer resources.

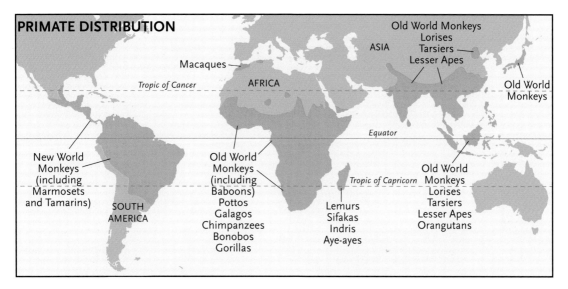

PRIMATE DISTRIBUTION

Old World Monkeys
Lorises
ASIA   Tarsiers
Lesser Apes

Macaques

Tropic of Cancer   AFRICA

Old World
Monkeys

Equator

New World
Monkeys
(including
Marmosets
and Tamarins)

SOUTH
AMERICA

Old World
Monkeys
(including
Baboons)
Pottos
Galagos
Chimpanzees
Bonobos
Gorillas

Tropic of Capricorn

Lemurs
Sifakas
Indris
Aye-ayes

Old World
Monkeys
Lorises
Tarsiers
Lesser Apes
Orangutans

Nonhuman primates are native to Africa, Asia, and Central and South America. Humans are the only primates that have managed to colonize all of the world's continents and most of its islands.

South America's savannah-dwelling primates are various species of capuchins, howler monkeys, titi monkeys, and marmosets. They live not on the grasslands but in the scattered patches of forests that dot the grasslands. In Africa, vervet, grivet, and patas monkeys occupy similar habitat. So do baboons, which also live on rocky hillsides and in scrub desert. On the island of Madagascar, a few species of lemurs have adapted to life in the thorn forests of the south—dry regions with sparse, thorny trees. In Asia, the primates most likely to be found in open woodland and savannah habitat are certain species of langurs and macaques.

Most primates live in very hot climates, but a few species have adapted to living in cold conditions. Hanuman langurs have been seen at altitudes of up to 13,200 feet (4,000 meters) above sea level on the lower slopes of the Himalayas, where temperatures sometimes fall below freezing. The yellow-tailed woolly monkey lives almost equally high on the slopes of South America's Andes Mountains. Certain galagos in the highlands of South Africa endure brief periods of freezing temperatures. The primate that occupies the

A golden snub-nosed monkey and its young in a Chinese wildlife reserve. These monkeys live higher in mountains and endure colder temperatures than any other nonhuman primate species.

highest—and therefore the coldest—altitude is the snub-nosed monkey of southwestern China. It lives in mountain forests up to 14,850 feet (4,500 meters) above sea level, with several months of snow and freezing temperatures each winter.

Macaques in the Snow

The primate that lives farthest from the warm tropics is the monkey species *Macaca fuscata*. This macaque inhabits the mountains of Japan, where winter brings cold days, colder nights, and occasionally heavy snow. Several adaptations, both physical and behavioral, help the macaques survive in this environment. One physical adaptation is their coat of hair, which becomes denser during the winter for extra warmth. Another is a digestive system that can get nourishment from a high-fiber diet of leaves, roots, and tree bark, which the macaques eat in wintertime when the fruits and vegetables they prefer are unavailable. Winter brings a change in behavior, too—the monkeys stay closer together by day and night for added warmth. Some Japanese macaques living near hot springs have even learned to soak in their steaming water during the winter. Primatologists are studying these monkeys to learn if they bathe in the springs only for warmth when temperatures plunge, or if they bathe at other times as well, which would suggest that they have learned to enjoy nature's hot tubs.

Some Japanese macaques soak in hot springs during cold winter weather. These macaques are sometimes called the "snow monkeys" of Japan.

FINDING FOOD

Primatologists today know more about what primates eat than they did twenty or even ten years ago. They have discovered that the diets of most primates are more varied than zoologists used to think. Even primates that specialize in or prefer one kind of food generally eat other things from time to time. Those that dine mostly on fruit, for example, also need protein, which they get by occasionally eating leaves and insects.

Depending upon the species, primates eat leaves, grasses, buds and flowers, seeds and nuts, fruits, honey, tree sap or gum, eggs, insects, and animals—including, sometimes, other primates. Many are fruit eaters, and

they play a key role in the life cycles of tropical forests. They discharge fruit seeds in their feces, often far from the tree where they ate the original fruit. This helps fruit-bearing plant species reproduce and spread.

Very few primates eat only plant materials or only animals. The tarsiers of Asia are the only strict carnivores, or meat eaters, in the primate world. They hunt at night, swiveling their ears to pick up the faint rustlings of insects, rotating their heads far around to pinpoint the location of every sound, peering through the darkness with their large

A male red uakari feeds on fruit in the Amazon region of Brazil.

eyes, and then seizing their prey with sharp little teeth. Tarsiers feed not only on cockroaches and other insects but on spiders, scorpions, snakes (including poisonous ones), bats, and small birds.

Galagos also eat insects and small animals, but their diet also includes fruit and the gums and saps that seep from trees and shrubs. Lorises, too, like animal prey, but they are slower-moving than tarsiers and galagos. Rather than pouncing swiftly, the loris creeps up quietly and favors prey that moves slowly or not at all, such as snails and birds' eggs. Lorises and pottos have evolved digestive systems that can handle beetles and other insects avoided by most predators because they taste terrible or even contain poison. Lemurs mix insects, small animals, eggs, fruit, flowers, buds, and gums in their diet. Dwarf lemurs have been known to prey on frogs almost their own size. The aye-aye is a specialized insectivore, or insect-eater, using its front teeth to chisel through bark and its long claw to pull out grubs, which are plump, wormlike insect larvae. Once commonly compared to a woodpecker and thought to eat nothing but insects found in trees, the aye-aye is now known to consume plant foods occasionally, using its claw to pull pulp from inside coconuts and other fruits.

Many monkeys are vegetarians—almost. The leaf-eating or colobine monkeys of Africa and Asia mostly eat leaves, as might be expected, but various species include seeds or fruit in their diets. Some occasionally also eat insects and spiders. Tamarins in Central and South America feast chiefly on fruit but also catch and eat small animals, such as lizards, frogs, and young birds. Gorillas live mostly on the leaves, shoots, and stems of plants such as bamboo. Sometimes, though, they tear into termite nests to eat the termites and their grubs.

Baboons and chimpanzees are true omnivores, which means that they eat both meat and plant foods in varying quantities depending upon what is available. The gelada of Ethiopia in East Africa is a grass-eater, using its opposable thumb to pick grass stems and seeds. When grasshoppers are numerous, however, the gelada eats as many of them as its can catch. When all else fails, it digs for roots. Baboons willingly eat meat and have been

Many primates, including this squirrel monkey, get their protein in the form of insect snacks.

known to chase, capture, and devour small mammals. On the South African coast they gather crabs and clams. Coastal macaques also hunt and eat crabs.

Chimpanzees also eat a wide variety of plant foods but also devour meat. Scientists have observed and even filmed groups of chimps pursuing prey such as red colobus monkeys, baboons, or young wild pigs. The victims are torn apart and shared among the hunters. Chimpanzees sometimes use sticks as weapons for striking their prey.

Chimpanzees are the only nonhuman primates that regularly use tools to obtain food. Some tree-dwelling monkeys crack nuts by banging two nuts together, but this method is time-consuming and not very efficient—a certain percentage of nuts either won't open or simply fall to the ground. Chimps, who spend much time on the ground, have a better method. They use rocks to crack the nuts, carefully choosing rocks that are heavy enough to do the job but not so heavy that they crush the meat inside the nut or become hard to

A chimpanzee uses a twig to fish for insects in a hollow log. Tool use is just one of many similarities between humans and our closest primate relatives.

lift. Chimpanzees also fish—for termites. To get a protein-rich meal of termites without the trouble of tearing apart the large, sturdy termite nest, a chimp may insert a stick into the nest entrance, wait until termites swarm onto the stick, and then pull it out and eat the catch. These fishing sticks are true tools. Chimps do not merely select them for the right length and thickness. They also prepare them for the job by removing leaves or twigs. Chimpanzees are resourceful and intelligent primates, able to figure out how to eat well with less work. Some of them have even found a stingless method of getting honey from bees' nests—insert a fishing stick, then simply lick off the sweet treat. Chimpanzees teach their young to use fishing sticks and rocks.

Primates eat plants as medicine, not just as food. Chimpanzees in East Africa, for example, chew the leaves of the aspilia plant—a plant that African people have used in traditional medicines for a long time. During the 1980s scientists discovered that aspilia contains chemicals that help fight some diseases. Researchers in Brazil have also found examples of primates using plants as medicine.

Ring-tailed lemurs playing with young in Madagascar.

Reproduction and Behavior

Many primates, especially the anthropoids, are social animals. They spend their lives with families, mates, troops of foraging partners, or even complex communities. Much of what primates do is geared toward communicating, competing for power, or simply getting along with others in their social circle.

REPRODUCTION

Compared with most other mammals, primates are slow breeders. Their gestation periods—the time during which unborn young develop inside their mother's body—are longer than for other mammals of similar size. Primates also have small families. Marmosets and tamarins usually have twins. Some prosimians bear two or three young, others have just one. Tarsiers, apes, and Old World monkeys have a single offspring at a time, although on rare occasions twins are born to great apes.

Primate young are born fairly helpless and require long periods of care. Primates are weaned later than other similar-sized mammals (weaning is the point at which a young mammal stops receiving milk from its mother's body). Young spider monkeys have lived for nearly three years—about one-seventh of their lives—by the time they are weaned. Chimpanzees, which live to an average of forty-one years in the wild, may not be completely weaned until the age of five. Intervals between births are also long—up to five and a half years for chimpanzees. All of this adds up to the fact that primate populations grow slowly.

Reproduction begins with mating, which happens only when a female enters a state of readiness called estrus. The timing of estrus varies widely from group to group. For most female prosimians it occurs once each year, at the same time for all members of each species. These animals have a regular mating season, which lasts anywhere from a single day to two weeks, and a birthing season, during which all pregnant females deliver their young. Tarsiers and a handful of other prosimians, however, have two periods of estrus each year. Most monkeys and all apes can breed at any time of year. Their females enter estrus not on a seasonal schedule but after they have weaned their previous young.

A female primate who is ready to mate signals her condition by releasing a special scent from her sexual organs or other glands. In some Old World monkey species, the skin around the sexual organs also becomes swollen or brightly colored. Males respond to these signals according to the mating behavior of each species.

Some primates are monogamous, which means that a male and female mate only with each other. Gibbons, indris, marmosets and tamarins, night monkeys, and titi monkeys appear to form monogamous pairs. A more common arrangement is for one male to mate with a number of females. In some species, several females and their young live in a troop with one male. Other species form groups containing multiple females and males, but often only the senior, or dominant, male gets to mate with the females. This is true of gorillas—a silverback dominates each group, and any other male who wants mating privileges must either take control from the silverback or form its own group. Still another arrangement has multiple males and females living together in large groups, as with capuchin monkeys, and forming a variety of mating patterns—sometimes, it seems, based simply on personal preference rather than on status within the group. In some species, such as chacma baboons, males fight for mating rights when a female comes into estrus. Barbary macaques and chimpanzees have a different strategy: Females choose their partners, and during estrus they may mate with many different males.

Prosimian mothers give birth to their young in nests, which may be tree holes or beds of branches and leaves. They are the only primates that make nests, although some anthropoids gather leaves into temporary sleeping cushions. Almost all primates, however, carry their young about with them from a very early age—in some cases, from immediately after birth. Primate young are born with strong grasping instincts in fingers and toes to

A young squirrel monkey travels with a parent through the Costa Rican rain forest. One of the first things many young primates learn to do is grip their parents' fur and hang on tightly.

help them clutch the fur of the adult's back or stomach. The mother is usually the carrier, but father marmosets, tamarins, and titi monkeys carry their young, sometimes more than the mothers do. Among both prosimians and anthropoids, however, the young of some species may be carried and cared for by older siblings, aunts, grandmothers, or even unrelated adults. Orphaned young may be adopted by unrelated adults, and there have even been primate kidnappings, in which one female steals a young infant from a smaller or weaker female and treats it as her own.

Some young primates are at risk of being murdered. In species in which females mate with more than one male, or in cases in which a new male takes over the dominant position in a troop, infanticide—the killing of infants or unweaned young—is fairly common. A male kills a female's young in order to bring her into estrus so that he can mate with her. This does not always happen, however. Male primates often tolerate and occasionally even nurture the offspring of other males.

SOCIAL LIFE

Most primates live in social groups. For a long time scientists believed that nocturnal primates, which normally forage alone, were solitary animals. New studies have shown, however, that tarsiers, bushbabies, and lemurs that spend much of their time alone also form social bonds, including shared or overlapping territories or group sleeping during the day. The orangutan is the only diurnal primate that follows a generally solitary way of life, with males and females coming together only to mate. Female orangs and their young remain together until the young are weaned, but otherwise adults live on their own, although they sometimes gather temporarily in loose groups. A particularly abundant food resource, such as a stand of fig trees, may attract several orangutans. They appear to get along, even at close quarters, by ignoring one another most of the time.

The complex social arrangements of other primates are the subject of hundreds of books and scientific articles. Social behavior varies dramatically among different types of primates. All kinds of group interaction, however, have two common features: training and communication.

One of the most important tasks of any young primate is to learn the rules that govern social interaction among its own kind. It does so by watching its mother and other adults and eventually copying their behavior. Play is another form of training that helps prepare a young primate for its role in society. At the heart of most—but not all—primate societies is a dominance hierarchy, a ladder of power and status. Dominant animals have power over those below them, called submissives. They may show their clout by controlling mating privileges; by eating first or the most, or getting

Young Japanese macaques playing. Primate play often involves mock fighting and wrestling. Such play helps the youngsters develop physical strength, but it also teaches them the skills they will need to interact with other animals in their communities.

the choicest tidbits; by leading the group as its forages; or by disciplining other members. Sometimes one female dominates the other females and the younger or lesser males but is submissive to the dominant male.

The importance of dominance in everyday life differs from species to species, and the hierarchy or status ladder is flexible and ever-changing. Young primates of some species "inherit" status from their mothers. Others establish their own status among other youngsters through play-fighting. As they get older, they can gain real dominance in the group as a whole by winning fights or, in the case of females, by bearing young. When an older primate loses a fight, however, it also loses dominance.

All primates are territorial to some degree. For some species, this simply means that they live and forage within a certain area. Scent from their odor glands as well as from their urine and feces signals their presence, so that other individuals and troops stay out of their way. A male's territory

Bonobo or pygmy chimpanzee troop.

may overlap that of several females, females may share all or part of a territory, or different troops may use the same territory at different times. Other primates, however, are more aggressive about keeping others out of their territories. Chimpanzees, in particular, engage in territorial violence. Chimp bands have been known to patrol the borders of their own range and to kill chimpanzee outsiders who enter. They also attack neighboring groups, sometimes killing or driving off all of the males and taking over the range. Chimpanzees may use branches or rocks as weapons in these battles. They are the only primates other than humans that make deliberate, armed, group raids into the home territory of other members of their own species, hunting and killing members of the "enemy" tribe.

Not all fights are physical and violent. Often, in confrontation, primates bare or snap their teeth, utter loud sounds or hisses, stand tall and wave their arms, slap the ground, or simply charge or chase one another. These actions are all forms of communication. Primates are excellent communicators, and they use scent, sound, and body language to send messages.

A primate's scent holds a wealth of information about its age, gender, and reproductive status. Animals that know each other can recognize each by scent—even newborn young recognize the scent of their mother. Depending upon the species, primates leave their scent in urine, feces, or scent markings from special glands in the hands, feet, face, forearms, or near the sexual organs.

Body language and behavior also communicate a variety of meanings beyond threat displays. Lip smackings, wide-open mouths, and heads tilted to the side usually indicate curiosity, friendliness, or a desire to play. A relaxed face and body signal a general good mood. Grinning, however, can be a sign of fear, aggression, or both. Another sign of aggression is a direct eye-to-eye stare. In Old World monkeys with tails, such as rhesus monkeys, the posture of the tail is a language in itself. Dominant monkeys hold their tails higher than submissive monkeys.

Grooming is another form of communication, one that strengthens connections among family or troop members. It usually begins when one animal approaches another, often in crouching posture to show that its intentions are not hostile, and presents itself to be groomed. The groomer picks through the first animal's hair, removing dirt, twigs, and parasites such as fleas and lice. All primates spend at least some time grooming one another, even if only among mothers and offspring or mating pairs.

Most primates also vocalize, or use sound to communicate. Their sounds can be fairly quiet, such as the murmurs, chirps, or hoots that mothers use to reassure their young. Troop members may use similar vocalizations to keep in touch with one another as they spread out through the branches or grass to forage. Some primates, however, have extremely loud vocalizations. Foraging groups of gibbons get louder and louder as they approach each other. The din increases until one group retreats. Howler monkeys, as you might expect from their name, are also noisy.

Rhesus macaques grooming, an important part of family and group life for many primates. Rhesus macaques, often called rhesus monkeys, are widely used in medical and scientific research. Laboratory rhesus macaques are seldom taken from the wild—they are raised in captive colonies specifically for research purposes.

Male black howler monkey. American traveler and adventure writer Arthur O. Friel visited South American in the 1920s and described the cries of the howler monkey as "louder and eerier than a thousand laughing hyenas."

Their booming roars echo across great distances in the early morning and again in the evening. Scientists think that these loud calls are the howler troops' way of taking roll call. Howlers also make a racket as they move through the trees foraging.

Some of the most interesting vocalizations are those of vervet monkeys, which scientists have studied closely on the African savannah. Many primates have alarm calls, special vocalizations to warn family or troop members when danger looms. Vervets, though, use different alarm calls for each of their three main predators. A vervet that sees an approaching eagle utters a call. Other vervets recognize the nature of the threat and flee from the treetops into lower branches where the eagle cannot get them. But if a vervet spots a leopard, it uses a different call. The others respond by scampering high into the trees, onto small branches that will not hold the big cat's weight. Finally, the snake call causes vervets to stay where they are but look around them carefully. These distinctive calls amount to a basic form of language. Primatologists are beginning to find that many other species also have specific vocalizations for certain circumstances.

In a very few cases, primates have gone beyond one-sound vocalizations to use language the way people use it, combining nouns, verbs, and adjectives to express ideas. Primates cannot speak human languages because the anatomy of their throats and mouths differs from that of people. However, the four great ape species appear to have the mental properties

Vervet monkeys are among the most effective communicators in the primate order. They use special calls to warn each other of different kinds of predators.

Dr. Sue Savage-Rumbaugh has taught bonobos to communicate using symbols that the apes learn and then arrange to form sentences.

needed to use human languages. Trainers have taught forms of language to captive gorillas, orangutans, chimpanzees, and bonobos. Some of these animals use the hand gestures of American Sign Language (ASL, used by many deaf people). Others have mastered the meanings of hundreds of symbols; they string "words" together by pointing to a series of symbols.

Repeated studies have shown that these "speaking" apes do not just repeat things but actually form new combinations of their own. Although some combinations are random and meaningless, quite a few are meaningful, such as accurate descriptions of things the "speakers" see around them. Although very few primates have learned to use language in this way, most of those have improved steadily with practice. And, in a development that surprised scientists, several have taught sign language to others of their species. These apes' ability to speak to us is a reminder that we are all primates together.

Native to Vietnam, Cambodia, and Laos in Southeast Asia, the douc is one of many primate species in danger of extinction. The species has not recovered from the large-scale destruction of its habitat during the Vietnam War.

Primates in Peril

Primates, our closest relatives, are also one of the most endangered orders in the animal kingdom. According to the World Conservation Union (IUCN), which monitors the status of wildlife around the world and regulates the wildlife trade, 33 species or subspecies of primates are critically endangered, and another 59 are endangered. They are at risk from loss of habitat, from hunting, and from the taking of live animals from the wild.

Habitat loss is hitting primates hard because most of them live in tropical forest. Of all environments on the planet, tropical forest is perhaps under the most severe attack. A report by the World Resources Institute reveals that in the late 1990s as many as 40,000 square miles (10 million hectares) of tropical forest were being destroyed each year, either by logging or clearing the land for other uses such as farming. Deforestation hurts primates directly by eliminating the trees that provide their homes and food sources. It also hurts them indirectly, by crowding them into ever-smaller areas of surviving forest, where they have to compete for dwindling resources.

Deforestation also increases the hunting and killing of primates by people. In some parts of the world people have always hunted primates for food. As forests are cleared, more people arrive, and the hunting pressure increases—at least for a while, until the primates are gone. This has happened throughout Central and West Africa. Construction of new roads for

The Brazilian government is building a highway to link the Amazon River and the southern part of the country. Environmentalists fear that the highway will speed up habitat loss for primates and other wildlife in the Amazon region. The route of the highway is being deforested, and when completed it will bring increasing numbers of settlers and businesses into the area to clear land, cutting down still more forest.

logging has opened large areas of forest to hunters who target monkeys and apes, especially the larger species, as a desirable form of "bush meat." Not only does bush meat feed the logging crews, many urban Africans consider it a delicacy and support a booming—though often illegal—trade in primate meat. The killing of primates for food has had serious results. It has contributed to the spread among humans of viruses such as the HIV and Ebola viruses. Another side effect of deforestation is that when people plant fields and gardens in what were once forests, surviving primates may forage among their crops. Villagers and farmers frequently shoot primates as pests, even species that are supposed to be protected by environmental laws.

Hunting primates for food, or to protect food crops, is unfortunate but understandable. Another type of hunting, however, is inexcusable. Some primates are killed to provide items for the souvenir trade, such as skins, tooth necklaces, and stuffed monkeys. In a few places in Africa, tourists can buy gorilla skulls and hands, although the killing of these great apes is strictly illegal. Primates have also been slaughtered for folk "remedies" that have no medicinal value. China's snub-nosed monkey, for example, is still sought by some because of a belief that its fur offers protection from rheumatism or other diseases. In Thailand, the blood of leaf monkeys, sometimes mixed with whiskey, is thought to improve sexual energy. Superstition has also hurt the rare aye-aye of Madagascar. Some people there kill this harmless lemur on sight because they think it brings bad luck.

A final threat to wild primate populations is the capture of live animals, either for pets or for use as laboratory animals. Since the 1980s, scientific and conservation organizations around the world have led a movement to use primates from captive breeding colonies in biological and medical research. As a result, far fewer animals, especially of endangered species, are now taken for these purposes. However, some primates, particularly marmosets and tamarins, have had wild populations reduced by the trade in exotic pets.

Primates in Research

People are primates—which means that some other members of the primate order are a lot like people. This family resemblance has been useful to people, who have used primates as substitutes for humans in medical and scientific research. Unfortunately, it hasn't been very good for the primates.

It is sometimes difficult or even impossible to experiment on humans. But the brains, bodies, and nervous systems of monkeys and apes are similar to those of people in a lot of ways. For this reason, monkeys and apes make good stand-ins for humans in many experiments aimed at improving human life through medicine or science. Chimpanzees, the nonhuman primates that are closest to humans, are most desirable for experimentation, but many other kinds of primates have also served as research subjects. Some research projects simply study behavior, such as learning skills. The primates in these experiments may not lead natural lives, but they are only observed. Other projects, however, call for more disturbing treatment of the animals, such as injecting them with diseases or testing new medicines and surgical procedures on them.

Some people believe that all animal experimentation is wrong. Even people who don't object to experiments on mice or rats may be disturbed by accounts of experiments on primates, such as studies by the United States National Institutes of Health in the 1970s, in which scientists used machines to strike chimpanzees' heads with great force to see what kind of damage the impacts caused. More recently, doctors studying AIDS (Acquired Immunodeficiency Syndrome) infected thousands of chimpanzees with HIV, the virus that causes AIDS, hoping to learn more about the disease. The experiments led nowhere. Their only result was a population of infected chimps that could not be released or used for other tests.

Yet primate research has also produced medical and scientific benefits, such as the cure for a viral disease called kuru, insight into how addiction affects the brain, and promising medical treatments for dozens of other conditions and diseases that affect hundreds of thousands of people worldwide. Some people feel that such results justify the use of primates in research. Today, most countries have laws that govern experimentation on primates. These laws limit the taking of primates from wild populations and say that laboratory animals must receive decent care and, when possible, drugs for pain relief. The question of whether it is right to experiment on our closest relatives, however, stirs strong feelings. It is a controversy that is not likely to disappear.

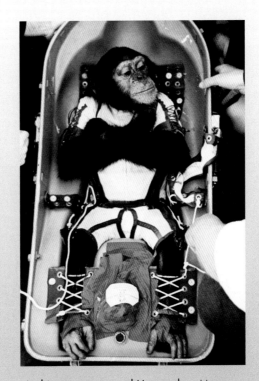

A chimpanzee named Ham rode a Mercury capsule into space in 1961, at the dawn of the United States space program. Unlike many primates who have been subjects of experiments, Ham survived the experience.

Monkeys for sale in Bali, Indonesia.

The IUCN regulates all international trade in wildlife and wildlife products and is trying to crack down on illegal shipments of primates or primate parts. In addition, governments in China, Africa, South America, and elsewhere have passed laws to protect at least some of their primate species. Such laws, however, are often poorly enforced, especially in remote rural regions. Political and economic events also effect conservation efforts, as shown by the plight of the mountain gorilla. During the 1980s, inspired by the widely publicized studies of gorilla researcher Dian Fossey, the African nation of Rwanda established a national park to protect its mountain gorillas. Park rangers tried to enforce laws against poaching, or illegal hunting, and tourists from around the world came to see the gorillas. Since that time, however, Rwanda has been torn by war and has suffered an economic crisis. Enforcement of the laws relaxed, and hunters began killing more gorillas. Although these apes are technically protected by law, their future is cloudy. Only a few hundred remain.

Wayne McGuire, an assistant of Dian Fossey, with some of the mountain gorillas that Fossey studied and fought to protect.

A handler works with western lowland gorillas in the Republic of the Congo. He is part of an effort to prepare orphaned or rescued gorillas for a return to life in the wild.

Primates' prospects are not all dark. International conservation organizations, including the World Wildlife Fund and the Nature Conservancy, are working with local governments and with grass-roots groups of local people to protect sections of habitat and the primates that live in them. Other conservation groups are devoted entirely to primates. They not only promote education about primates but raise funds for wildlife refuges and research stations around the world.

One strategy for long-term primate protection is to convince local populations that primates are worth more alive and in the wild than dead. A dead lemur, for example, is a meal, but live lemurs can attract visitors who will spend money on nature tours, lodging, and meals while they travel in Madagascar. A long-lasting ecological tourism industry in Rwanda should bring more money into the country than the skulls and hands of all the remaining mountain gorillas. At the same time, primatologists hope that the lemurs, monkeys, and apes of the world will never be reduced to nothing more than tourist attractions. Wild primates in their natural habitats, undisturbed by human activities, are a key part of many ecosystems. Scientists are continually discovering new things about them—and finding that they have still more to learn. Primates have been around for a long, long time. It would be tragic if one primate species drove the rest into extinction.

Ecotourism brings visitors from around the world face to face with primates—such as this young mountain gorilla—in their native habitats. Can ecotourism help save the remaining wild primates? Like much else about this amazing order of animals, the answer is not yet known.

adapt—To change or develop in ways that aid survival in the environment.

ancestral—Having to do with lines of descent or earlier forms.

anthropoid—Monkey or ape.

arboreal—Living in trees.

brachiation—The act of swinging by the arms from handhold to hand hold, turning the body from side to side with each swing.

conservation—Action or movement aimed at saving or preserving wildlife or its habitat.

deforestation—Loss of tree cover through natural means, such as fire or climate change, or through human activities, such as logging or clearing forests for construction or farming.

diurnal—Active during the day.

dominant—Having more status or power in the hierarchy.

evolution—Process by which new species, or types of plants and animals, emerge from old ones over time.

evolve—To change over time.

extinct—No longer existing; died out.

forage—To look for food.

genetic—Having to do with genes, material made of DNA inside the cells of living organisms. Genes carry information about inherited characteristics from parents to offspring.

gestation—Period between fertilization and birth, during which mammal offspring develop inside the mother's body.

habitat—Type of environment in which an animal lives.

hierarchy—Ladder or ranking. Primate communities have a status hierarchy, with one or more individuals on top and descending levels of status below.

mammal—Animal with a backbone that nourishes its young with milk from its mammary glands. All primates are mammals, as are hundreds of other animals.

naturalist—Someone who studies nature; early term for biologist or other scientist interested in the natural world.

nocturnal—Active during the night.

organism—Any living thing.

paleontologist—A scientist who studies ancient or extinct life forms, usually through fossils.

prehensile—Capable of grasping, holding, or picking up objects. Some primates have prehensile tails that they use as extra hands.

primate—A member of the group of animals that includes prosimians, monkeys, apes, and humans.

primatologist—A scientist who specializes in the study of primates.

prosimian—Any primate that is not a monkey, an ape, or human, such as a lemur, galago, loris, or tarsier; sometimes called a lower primate.

savannah—Tropical or subtropical grassland with scattered trees.

simian—A monkey, or characteristic of monkeys.

submissive—Having less status or power in the hierarchy.

taxonomy—Scientific system for classifying living things, arranging them in categories according to similarities and differences, and naming them.

zoologist—A scientist who specializes in the study of animals.

Nonhuman Primate

STREPSIRHINES

 <u>Galagos</u> (or bushbabies)

 <u>Lorises</u>

 <u>Lemurs</u>
 True lemurs
 Sportive lemurs
 Dwarf or mouse lemurs
 Indrids
 Aye-ayes

Apes

<u>Great Apes</u>
Orangutans
Chimpanzees
Bonobos or pygmy chimps
Gorillas

<u>Lesser Apes</u>
Gibbons
Siamangs

<u>Cercopithecines</u>
Guenons, Vervets, Forest monkeys
Patas monkeys
Mangabeys
Baboons and Mandrills
Geladas
Macaques

Family Tree

HAPLORHINES

Monkeys

Tarsiers

Old World

New World
Marmosets and Tamarins
Atelids
Cebids

Colobines
Colobuses
Langurs
Proboscis monkeys
Doucs
Snub-nosed or golden monkeys

F U R T H E R   R E A D I N G

Barrett, Norman S. *Monkeys and Apes*. New York: Franklin Watts, 1988.

Grace, Eric S. *Apes*. San Francisco: Sierra Club Books for Children, 1995.

Hook, Patrick. *The World of Primates*. New York: Gramercy Books, 2000.

Lasky, Kathryn. *Shadows in the Dawn: The Lemurs of Madagascar*. San Diego: Harcourt Brace, 1998.

Martin, Patricia. *Lemurs, Lorises, and Other Lower Primates*. New York: Children's Press, 2000.

Saign, Geoffrey. *The Great Apes*. New York: Franklin Watts, 1998.

Smith, Roland. *Primates in the Zoo*. Brookfield, CT: Millbrook Press, 1992.

Stonehouse, Bernard. *A Visual Introduction to Monkeys and Apes*. New York: Checkmark Books, 2000.

WEB SITES

www.primate.wisc.edu/pin

The University of Wisconsin's Primate Research Center operates the Primate Information Network, an online source of scientific and conservation information, including a useful section on primate taxonomy, with links to and information about the various primate family trees that scientists have suggested in recent years.

www.indiana.edu/~primate/primates/html

The African Primates at Home site contains not only information about African primates but also scenes and sounds of primates in natural settings.

animaldiversity.ummz.umich.edu/chordata/mammalia/primates. html

The University of Michigan's Museum of Zoology presents its primate taxonomy, along with information about each family of primates.

www.ippl.org

The home page of the International Primate Protection League, which has worked since 1973 to protect primates around the world from poaching, habitat loss, and other threats.

www.talkorigins.org

Fossil Hominids: The Evidence for Human Evolution presents an overview of paleoanthropology, the study of human ancestors and evolution; features include links, a timeline, a list of the most important hominid fossils, and a response to the claims of antievolutionists.

The author found these books especially helpful when researching this volume.

Dolhinow, Phyllis and Agustin Fuentes, editors. *The Nonhuman Primates.* Mountain View, CA: Mayfield Publishing, 1999.

Dunbar, Robin. *Cousins: Our Primate Relatives.* New York: Dorling Kindersley, 2002.

Fleagle, John. *Primate Adaptation and Evolution.* San Diego: Academic Press, 1999.

Napier, J.R. and P.H. Napier. *The Natural History of the Primates.* Cambridge, MA: MIT Press, 1985.

Nowak, Ronald M. *Walker's Primates of the World.* Baltimore: Johns Hopkins University Press, 1999.

Preston-Mafham, Rod and Ken Preston-Mafham. *Primates of the World.* London: Blandford, 1999.

Richard, Alison F. *Primates in Nature.* New York: W.H. Freeman, 1985.

Rowe, Noel. *The Pictorial Guide to the Living Primates.* East Hampton, NY: Pogonias Press, 1996.

Sleeper, Barbara. *Primates: The Amazing World of Lemurs, Monkeys, and Apes.* San Francisco: Chronicle Books, 1997.

Swindler, Daris R. *Introduction to the Primates.* Seattle: University of Washington Press, 1998.

Tattersall, Ian. *Becoming Human: Evolution and Human Uniqueness.* New York: Harcourt Brace, 1998.

I N D E X

Page numbers in **boldface** are illustrations and charts.

Rebecca Stefoff is the author of a number of books on scientific subjects for young readers. She has explored the world of animals in Marshall Cavendish's Living Things series and in the volumes *Horses, Bears, Dogs, Cats* and *Tigers* in the AnimalWays series, also published by Marshall Cavendish. She has also written about evolution in *Charles Darwin and the Evolution Revolution* (Oxford University Press, 1996), and she appeared in the *A&E Biography* segment on Charles Darwin and his work. Stefoff lives in Portland, Oregon.